Opening a Bank Account

by Stuart Schwartz and Craig Conley

Consultant:
Robert J. Miller, Ph.D.
Professor of Special Education
Mankato State University

CAPSTONE BOOKS

an imprint of Capstone Press
Mankato, Minnesota

Capstone Books are published by Capstone Press
151 Good Counsel Drive, P.O. Box 669, Mankato, Minnesota 56002
http://www.capstone-press.com

Copyright © 1999 Capstone Press. All rights reserved.
No part of this book may be reproduced without written permission from the publisher. The publisher takes no responsibility for the use of any of the materials or methods described in this book, nor for the products thereof.
Printed in the United States of America.

Library of Congress Cataloging-in-Publication Data
Schwartz, Stuart, 1945–
    Opening a bank account/by Stuart Schwartz and Craig Conley.
    p. cm. — (Life skills)
    Includes bibliographical references and index.
    Summary: Explains the fundamental steps for opening a bank account, offers advice on choosing a bank and selecting a type of account, and discusses the various services available at a bank.
    ISBN 0-7368-0047-6
    1. Bank accounts—Juvenile literature. [1. Bank accounts. 2. Banks and banking. 3. Finance, Personal.] I. Conley, Craig, 1965- . II. Title. III. Series: Schwartz, Stuart, 1945– Life skills.
HG1660.A3S39   1999
332.1'752—dc21   98-35115
                                                                             CIP
                                                                              AC

Editorial Credits
Christy Steele, editor; James Franklin, cover designer and illustrator; Michelle L. Norstad, photo researcher

Photo credits
All photographs by Barb Stitzer Photography

Table of Contents

Chapter 1   Banks 5
Chapter 2   Choosing a Bank 7
Chapter 3   Opening a Bank Account 9
Chapter 4   Savings Accounts 11
Chapter 5   Checking Accounts 13
Chapter 6   Checks 15
Chapter 7   Writing Checks 17
Chapter 8   Account Registers 19
Chapter 9   Bank Statements 21
Chapter 10 Computers and Banking 23
Chapter 11 Other Bank Services 25
Chapter 12 Importance of Bank Accounts 27

Words to Know 28
To Learn More 29
Useful Addresses 30
Internet Sites 31
Index 32

Chapter 1

Banks

Banks are places where people keep their money. Banks lend money to people and help people keep track of their money. People who work in banks give customers advice about managing money.

Banks use the money that people keep in their accounts. Banks might loan this money to other people. Banks pay their customers a fee called interest for using the money. Interest rates are different at different banks.

A savings and loan is one kind of bank. Savings and loan banks lend money to people. People take loans to buy expensive things such as cars or houses. A credit union is another kind of bank. Large groups such as companies and labor unions form credit unions.

Most towns and cities have banks. Some banks have more than one office. They may have a main bank and branch offices. Customers can do business at any of these banks. Some banks have branch offices in many cities.

A bank is a place where people keep their money.

Chapter 2

Choosing a Bank

People should compare banks before choosing one. Many people choose the bank that offers the highest interest rates. Most banks offer the same basic services such as checking and savings accounts. Banks rent deposit boxes for keeping important papers and objects safe.

People should choose the bank that offers the most free services. Some banks offer free checking accounts while other banks charge fees. Some banks charge fees if the amount of money in an account falls below a certain amount. Some banks offer special services for senior citizens, teenagers, or college students.

The location of a bank is important. People should choose a bank they can reach easily. Banks near a person's home, work, or school are best.

People should ask friends and family members about the banks they use. This will help people find out more about other banks.

Some banks have special services for teenagers and college students.

Chapter 3

Opening a Bank Account

People must apply to open accounts at their chosen banks. Account representatives help new customers open bank accounts.

People must show personal identification to the account representatives. The new customers must prove that they are the person they claim to be. Most banks require two forms of identification, such as a driver's license or a social security card.

New customers must fill out bank forms with personal facts. People must give banks their social security numbers, phone numbers, addresses, and other information. Banks can then contact people about their accounts.

Some banks need a minimum deposit before they will open an account. A minimum deposit is the lowest sum of money a bank will hold in an account. It is usually a small amount.

People can conduct bank transactions after they open accounts. They can deposit money or withdraw money.

New customers must fill out bank forms.

Chapter 4

Savings Accounts

A savings account is one type of bank account. People use savings accounts to save money in a safe place. They save money for expensive things they want to buy.

People can withdraw money from their savings accounts when they need to. But most banks usually require customers to keep a minimum balance in their accounts. Banks may charge fees or close accounts if balances drop below the minimum balance.

Banks pay interest on money people keep in savings accounts. A savings account of $100 with a 5 percent interest rate will earn $5 per year. People should find out which bank offers the highest interest rates for savings accounts.

Account representatives help people open savings accounts. Account representatives explain how savings accounts work and answer any questions customers may have.

People use savings accounts to save money for expensive things they want to buy.

Chapter 5

Checking Accounts

A checking account is another type of bank account. People use the money in their checking accounts to pay for goods or services. Checking accounts are a safe way to pay for things people buy through the mail. It is not safe to send cash in the mail.

New customers receive some checks when they open checking accounts. A check is a piece of paper with a person's account number on it. A check authorizes a bank to pay out an amount of money from a person's account.

People should find out what fees banks charge. Some banks charge fees for checking accounts. Other banks only charge fees if people write many checks each month. And banks charge overdraft fees when people take too much money out of their accounts.

People should choose the banks that best meet their needs. Banks that pay interest and offer free checking accounts are usually good choices.

People use the money in their checking accounts to pay for goods or services.

Name
Address
Phone Number
Check Number
FRANCINE V. JOHNSON
502-96-5734
11321 HWY. 2 & 52 W. 838-3926
BURLINGTON, ND 58722
0296
77-25/913
6/4 19 98
Pay To The Order of Jeremy Burner
$ 20.00
ten dollars and 00/100 Dollars
FIRST AMERICAN BANK WEST
MINOT, ND 58702
VOID
For
Frannie Johnson
⑆0333000000⑆ 66⑈444⑈5⑈ 0296
ARTISTIC CHECKS® • 1-800-224-7621 • TROPICAL FISH
© 1995 ARTISTIC GREETINGS, INC.
FRANCINE V. JOHNSON
502-96-5734
11321 HWY. 2 & 52 W. 838-3926
BURLINGTON, ND 58722
0297
77-25/913
6/4 19 98
Pay To The Order of Jeremy Burner
$ 20.00
twenty dollars and 00/100 Dollars
FIRST AMERICAN BANK WEST
MINOT, ND 58702
For
Frannie Johnson
⑆0333000000⑆ 66⑈444⑈5⑈ 0297
ARTISTIC CHECKS® • 1-800-224-7621 • TROPICAL FISH
© 1995 ARTISTIC GREETINGS, INC.
Bank Number
Account Number
Check Number

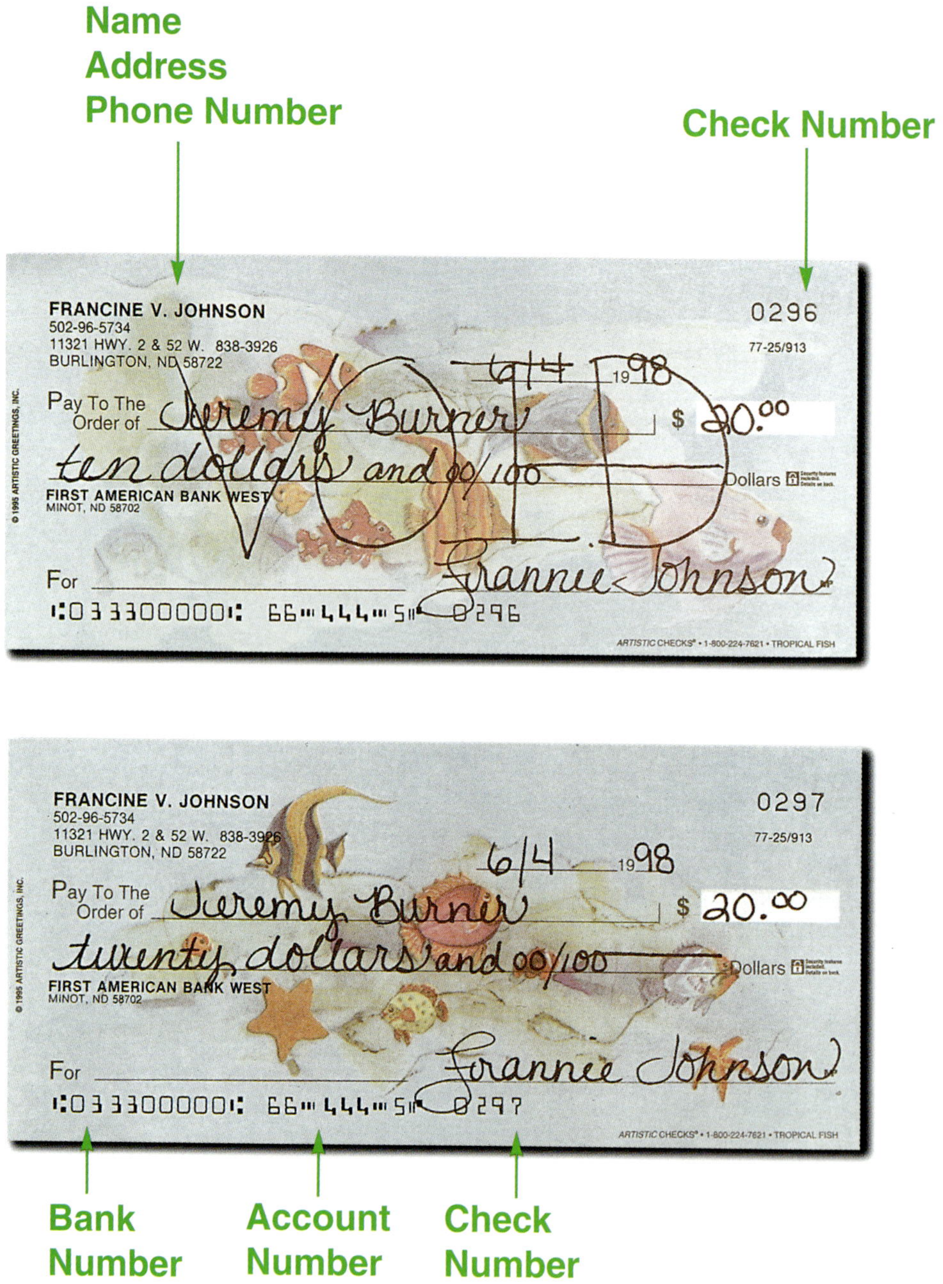

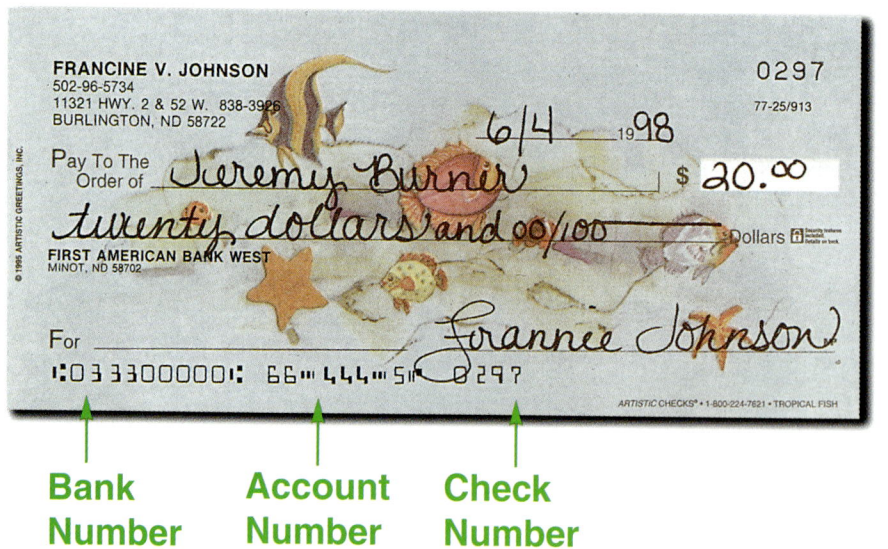

Chapter 6

Checks

People order checks when they open checking accounts. People choose what they want their checks to look like. Checks are available in many styles, colors, and backgrounds. People usually must pay for their checks. They fill out order forms with important facts. These facts are then printed on their checks.

People must make sure their checks have the correct facts. Printers might make mistakes. The person's name and address should be in the upper-left corner of the check. Some people have their telephone numbers and driver's license numbers on the checks too.

Checks are numbered so that banks can keep track of people's accounts. The number of each check is in the upper-right corner. The bank's number on the lower-left corner tells other banks where to send the check. The person's account number is next to the bank number. The check number appears a second time at the right of the account number. It usually has a zero in front of it.

Checks are available in many styles, colors, and backgrounds.

Chapter 7

Writing Checks

People must write each check correctly or the bank will not pay out the money. People should write the date on their checks. They must sign their names on the checks. They also must write the name of the store or the person receiving the check.

There is a place on every check to spell out the amount of money. For example, to write a check for $20, a person would write "twenty." A person should draw a line after the amount to the end of the space. This line prevents someone from adding words that make the check worth more. The person must also write the amount in numerals in the box on the right side of the check. The person would write "$20.00" in the box.

People should write "Void" across a check if they make a mistake. The word "Void" means that the check cannot be cashed. They should write "Void" beside that check's number in their register too. People use registers to keep a record of their accounts.

Chapter 8

Account Registers

All banks give information about accounts to new customers. Savings account customers receive savings books. Checking account customers receive checks and checkbooks. The books also contain registers and deposit or withdrawal slips.

People write their transactions in the registers. One column in the register is the balance column. The balance is the amount of money people have in the account. The balance changes when people deposit money or withdraw money. The balance also changes when people earn interest, write checks, or pay fees.

The deposit column and withdrawal column are other register columns. People should write the amount of their deposit in the deposit column. They should add the deposit amount to the balance. People should write the amount they withdraw in the withdrawal column. They should subtract the withdrawal amount from the balance. People who keep track of all their transactions always will know their balance.

People write their transactions in registers.

Chapter 9

Bank Statements

Banks keep track of each customer's transactions and account balance. The record of a person's account activity is called a bank statement. Banks send bank statements to their customers once every month.

Bank statements list the deposits and withdrawals people make each month. They list each check the bank has paid. Statements also list the dates of the transactions. People should make sure their register records match their bank statements. They should contact their bank if their statements and registers do not match. Banks can make mistakes.

Bank statements can be hard to understand. They show transactions only up to the date the statements were printed. Statements usually include directions that tell how to read them.

People should talk to bank representatives if they cannot understand their statements. Bank representatives can show their customers how to read bank statements.

People should make sure their register records match their bank statements.

Chapter 10

Computers and Banking

Many banks offer computer services to make transactions easier for customers. These banks give customers bank cards. People can use their bank cards at automated teller machines (ATMs) 24 hours a day. They can deposit money, withdraw money, or check their account balances at any time. ATMs are in many locations.

Banks assign a password to each person's account. Only the person with the account knows the password. People should not tell their passwords to others. People must keep their bank cards safe too. They should not give their cards to others. People must tell their bank if a bank card is lost or stolen.

Many banks accept direct deposits. Direct deposits are computer transactions. For example, employers transfer workers' paychecks through computers. Direct deposits can save people time.

People can use automated teller machines to deposit or withdraw money from their accounts.

Chapter 11

Other Bank Services

Some banks offer additional services to their customers. These banks might have programs that allow their customers to invest. For example, people might put money into other businesses. Then the people earn money if the businesses earn money.

Some banks lend money to their customers. Customers must pay interest fees to banks for such loans. Banks only lend money to people who show they can pay it back.

Another way banks lend money is by giving credit cards to customers. Customers can use credit cards instead of cash or checks to buy goods. The banks pay for the customers' credit-card purchases. Customers pay no interest if they pay back the entire amount each month. Otherwise, they must pay interest fees to the banks for their purchases.

Banks usually limit the amount people can charge on their credit cards. This limit depends on how much the customer earns each year. People should know their credit-card limits.

Some banks offer additional services to their customers.

Chapter 12

Importance of Bank Accounts

Bank accounts make it easy to keep track of money. A savings account can help people save money. Checking accounts make it easy to pay bills.

But a bank account is a big responsibility. People should be careful when handling their accounts. They must always write down how much money they deposit and they withdraw.

People also are responsible for protecting their bank accounts. People should keep their account numbers secret. They must keep their credit cards and bank cards in a safe place. They should keep checkbooks and unused checks in a safe place too. Checks are worthless until people sign them, so people must never sign checks in advance.

People should call their banks immediately if they lose their bank cards or checkbooks. Banks can stop payments on checks and charges. People will not have to pay unless they wrote the checks or made the charges.

People must always keep track of how much money they deposit and withdraw.

Words to Know

account (uh-KOUNT) — an arrangement to keep money in a bank

balance (BAL-uhnss) — the total amount of money in an account

credit union (KRED-it YOON-yuhn) — a bank set up by a group

deposit (di-POZ-it) — an amount of money added to an account

identification (eye-den-tuh-fuh-KAY-shuhn) — something that proves who a person is

investment (in-VEST-mint) — an amount of money lent or given to something such as a business in the belief that you will get more money back in the future

transaction (tran-ZAK-shuhn) — an exchange of money or services

void (VOID) — a word written on checks to make them worthless

withdrawal (with-DRAW-uhl) — an amount of money taken out of an account

To Learn More

Armentrout, Patricia. *Paying Without Money.* Money. Vero Beach, Fla.: Rourke Press, 1996.

Bungum, Jane E. *Money and Financial Institutions.* Economics for Today. Minneapolis: Lerner Publications, 1991.

Dunnan, Nancy. *Banking.* The Inside Track Library. Englewood Cliffs, N.J.: Silver Burdett Press, 1990.

Patten, John M., Jr. *Numbers and Money.* Read All about Numbers. Vero Beach, Fla.: Rourke Publications, 1996.

Sobczak, Joan. *Banking.* Money and Me. Vero Beach, Fla.: Rourke Publications, 1997.

Useful Addresses

America's Community Bankers
900 19th Street NW
Suite 400
Washington, DC 20006

Canadian Bankers Association
Commerce Court West, Suite 3000
199 Bay Street
Toronto, Ontario M5L 1G2
Canada

Institute of Canadian Bankers
Tour Scotia
1002 Sherbrooke Street West
Suite 1000, 10th Floor
Montreal, Quebec H3A 3M5
Canada

National Banking Network
2628 Barrett Street
Virginia Beach, VA 23452

Internet Sites

BankWeb
http://www.bankweb.com

Canadian Financial Sites
http://maestro.uwaterloo.ca/~cbilodea/finance.html

Consumer Banking Guide
http://www.banksite.com

Worldwide Banking Guide
http://www.worldpub.com/banks/index.asp

Index

automated teller machine (ATM), 23

bank card, 23, 27
bank statement, 21
branch offices, 5

check, 13, 15, 17, 19, 27
checking account, 7, 13, 19, 27
credit cards, 25, 27
credit union, 5

deposit boxes, 7
deposit slip, 19
direct deposits, 23

fees, 13, 19

interest, 5, 7, 11, 13, 19, 25

invest, 25

location, 7, 23

minimum balance, 11
minimum deposit, 9

overdraft fees, 13

personal identification, 9

register, 17, 19, 21

savings account, 7, 11, 19, 27
savings and loan, 5

void, 17